KEY STAGE 3 MATHEMATICS
Paper 1/2

PRACTICE TEST 1

Time :
Total time for this test is 1 hour.

Instructions :
Write your name in the space below.
Write your answers in the spaces
provided in the paper.
Check your work carefully.

Information :
Total mark for this Test is 66.
Numbers in brackets at the end of
each question indicate the marks awarded
to each answer or part of an answer.

Mark	
Total	66 (Maximum)

Pupil Name :

_____

1.   Here are 4 numbered cards.

a.   One of the numbers is the product
of two of the other three.
Which number is it ?

Answer _____   [1]

b.   What is the product of
all 4 numbers ?

Answer _____   [1]

c.   Which of the 4 numbers is both
a cubic and a square number ?

Answer _____   [1]

2.   Fill in the missing numbers for the function machine below.

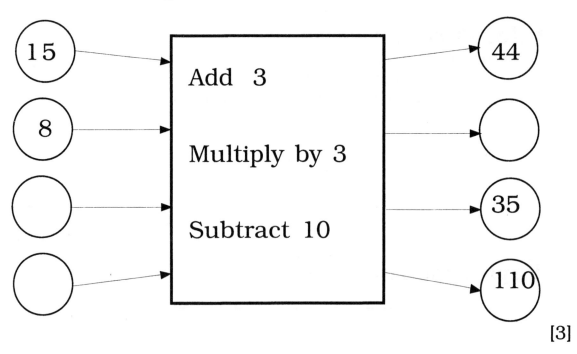

[3]

2.

SHOW ALL YOUR WORKING

3.   Harry, Alan and Paul go into a restaurant for lunch. Part of the menu is shown here.

MENU	
Soup	85p
Stew	£1.95
Roll	37p
Chips	£1.10
Burger	£1.65
Milk	72p
Coke	95p

a.   Alan spends **£2 . 32** on two items.
What does he buy ?

Answer _____ and

_____   [2]

b.   Paul pays **£3 . 60** for his lunch.
Which 3 items did he buy ?

Answer _____,_____ and

_____ .   [2]

c.   Harry was hungry so he bought all the items on the Menu.
How much change had he out of £20 ?

Answer £ _____   [1]

4.   a.   March 23rd 2001 was on a
Monday. What was the date
of the next Monday in March ?

Answer _____   [1]

b.   Which day of the week was the
last day of February 2001 ?

Answer _____   [1]

c.   What date in April was the
first Monday of April 2001?

Answer _____   [1]

5.   Below is a drawing of a Big Wheel at a Fun Park.
Gale is in the carriage **D**. The wheel moves in a clockwise
direction through ' **three-quarters** ' of a revolution.

   a.   With an **X** mark where carriage **D** would be after the move. [2]

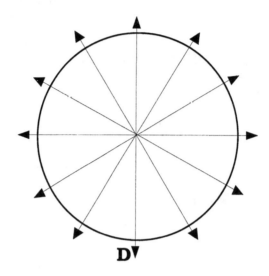

D

   b.   Through what angle did the big wheel
turn as carriage **D** moved to **X** ?

Answer _____° [1]

6.   a.   Mark was selling £6 tickets for a charity.
He sold 15 tickets each day.
How many did he sell in a fortnight ?

Answer _____ tickets [1]

   b.   Mark had to raise £1000.
How many tickets did he have to
sell to reach his target ?

Answer _____ tickets [2]

SHOW ALL YOUR WORKING

7. Write the missing numbers in the spaces to complete the sums below.

a.
```
    1   3   7
+   □   □   □
_____
    2   1   4
```
[1]

b.
```
    □   □   □
+       8   9
_____
    3   3   3
```
[1]

8. Write the missing numbers in the spaces to complete the sums below.

a.
```
        5   9
X           □
_____
    4   1   3
```
[1]

b.
```
    □   □   □
X           6
_____
    7   1   4
```
[1]

9. Below is a number pattern.

2, 5, 11, 23,

a. What is the next number in this sequence ?

Answer _____ [1]

b. Write down a RULE for this sequence.

_____

_____ [1]

10. The flow chart is used to sort out numbers which are less than 50.

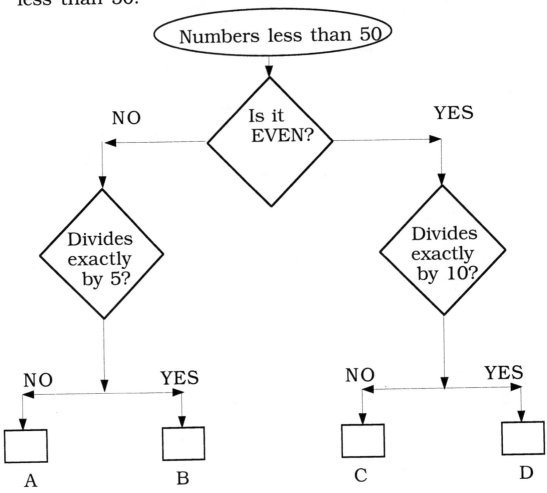

Use the flow diagram to sort out the following numbers:-

45   **32**   **20**   **17**

Write each number in the boxes A, B, C or D.   [2]

11. Change the following lengths into CENTIMETRES.

a.   45.6 millimetres   =   _____ cms   [1]

b.   9 milllimetres   =   _____ cms   [1]

c.   3.08 metres   =   _____ cms   [1]

d.   0.54 metres   =   _____ cms   [1]

SHOW ALL YOUR WORKING

12. Below are a number of triangles.

Work out the area of each and write it in the box below each triangle.

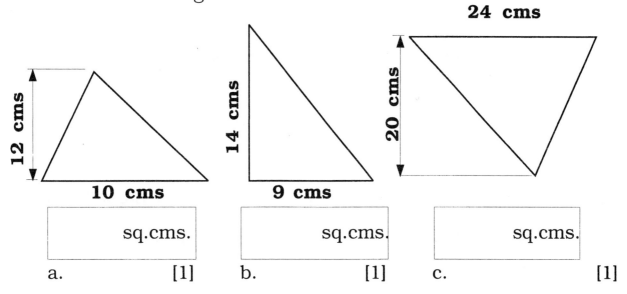

sq.cms.	sq.cms.	sq.cms.
a. [1]	b. [1]	c. [1]

13. a. 75 millimetres is approximately

    1 inch   1 foot   3 inches   7.5 inches   1 yard

    Circle your answer.   [1]

    b. 1 foot is approximately

    30 cms   30 mm   1 metre   90 cms   100 cms

    Circle your answer.   [1]

14. a. What number is 100 times less than 11 ?

                Answer _____   [1]

    b. What number is 1000 greater than 0.07 ?

                Answer _____   [1]

15. a.   How many times is the **3** in **306**
          greater than the **3** in the number **763** ?

                                    Answer _____   [1]

b.   How many times is the **5** in **25** less than
          the **5** in the number **5624** ?

                                    Answer _____   [1]

16.   Sweets are packed into 2 sizes of cartons **LARGE** and **small.**

       The total weight of 2 large cartons and 8 small cartons
       is 22.4 kgs.

       A **LARGE** carton weighs 2.4 kgs.

       What is the weight of a small carton ?

                                    Answer _____ kgs   [2]

17.   The Martin family spent the following amounts on food for a 4
       week period.

       £45.88   £60.24   £42.00   £50.60

a.   What was the mean weekly
          food bill for the Martins ?

                                    Answer £ _____   [2]

b.   Their average weekly phone bill was £21.95.
          What was the total phone bill for the 4 weeks ?

                                    Answer £ _____   [2]

8.

SHOW ALL YOUR WORKING

18. In a bicycle race the riders were wearing numbers from **6** to **40**.

a. If the winner was wearing a number which is a multiple of **8** and a number which is a **square number**, what was the number on the winner's jersey ?

Answer _____ [1]

b. The runner-up in the race wore a jersey with a number which was a factor of **40**. Write down all the numbers which could have been worn.

Answer _____ [1]

c. The last rider to cross the finishing line wore a number which is the **highest prime number** . Write down this number.

Answer _____ [1]

19. A scooter travels 17.3 kms on 1 litre of petrol. A 250cc motorbike travels 13.5kms on 1 litre of petrol.

a. Which of the two machines will travel further on 5 litres of petrol and by how many kms ?

Answer _____

_____ kms [2]

b. The Motorbike does a journey of 270 kms. How many litres of petrol does it need for this journey ? Show your working.

Answer _____ litres [2]

20. Below are some **"Measures Sentences"** with missing measurements.

Complete the sentences .

a.   15 Kgs **+** 750 grams   =   _ _ _ _ _ _ _ _ _ grams   [1]

b.   125 grams **+** 425 Kgs   =   _ _ _ _ _ _ _ _ _ grams   [1]

c.   _ _ _ _ _ _ _ _ kgs   _   2500 grams = 5.5 kgs   [1]

d.   7.75 kgs   _ _ _ _ _ _ _ _ _ _ _ grams = 4.1 15 kgs   [1]

21.   Which of the following is the drawing of a net of a cube.

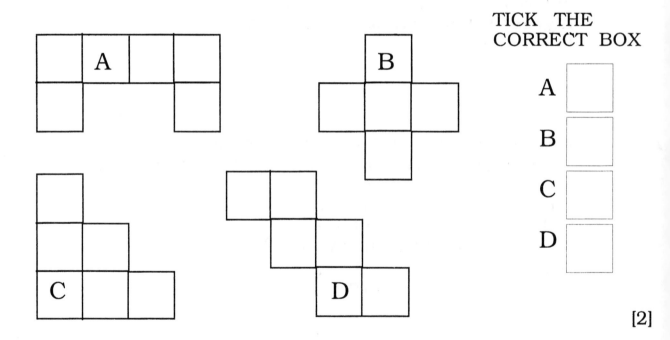

TICK THE
CORRECT BOX

A [ ]

B [ ]

C [ ]

D [ ]

[2]

22.   Mary has three £1 coins, two 50p coins and six 20p coins.

She buys a toy costing £4.55.

How much money has she left ?

Answer £ _____   [1]

SHOW ALL YOUR WORKING

23. Below is part of an Airline timetable for 4 plane journeys.

Complete the table giving your answers as 24-hour times.

	Flight Number	Departure time	Length of flight	Arrival Time
a.	MB 98	0715	4hrs. 50 mins	
b.	MB 111	1030	10 hrs	
c.	MB 92	1225		1640
d.	MB 99		5 hrs. 35 mins	2310
e.	MB 90	2020		2300

[2]

24. The given Circle is to be divided

into a Spinner with 4 sections

for the following colours, PINK,

BLACK, WHITE and GREEN.

The Spinner is divided so that :

the chance of scoring

BLACK is **greatest**

the chance of scoring PINK is **least** and

the chance of scoring GREEN and WHITE is the **same**.

The WHITE section has been done.

Divide up the Spinner and label it
with PINK, BLACK and GREEN.

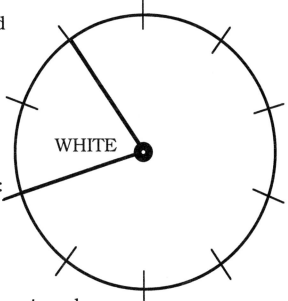

[3]

PTQ Tuition
Practice Materials
Tel: 02879632342

KEY STAGE 3 MATHEMATICS Paper 3

PRACTICE TEST 2

Time :
Total time for this test is 1 hour.

Instructions :
Write your name in the space below.
Write your answers in the spaces
provided in the paper.
Check your work carefully.

Information :
Total mark for this Test is 66.
Numbers in brackets at the end of
each question indicate the marks awarded
to each answer or part of an answer.

Mark	
Total	66 (Maximum)

Pupil Name :

_____

1.   An unknown number is represented by the letter **p**.

If **p - 6 = 4** :-

a.   What is the number value of **p** ?

Answer _____   [1]

b.   What is the number value of **3p + 3** ?

Answer_____   [1]

c.   What is the number value of **"p-cubed** " ?

Answer_____   [1]

2.   This brick design is for a boundary wall around a house.

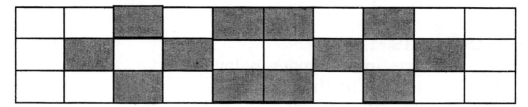

a.   What is the Ratio in lowest terms
of the Textured bricks to Plain bricks ?

Answer _____:_____   [1]

b.   What % of this pattern are the Textured bricks ?

Answer _____%   [2]

c.   If the Total number of bricks needed to
build the complete boundary wall is
1200 how many of these would be Textured bricks ?

Answer _____   [2]

2.

3. A large window manufacturer makes deliveries across the whole of Ireland. Below is a distance table for 5 major locations for delivery.

Belfast				
176	Dublin			
380	220	Cork		
250	175	95	Limerick	
180	205	190	170	Sligo

a.   What is the distance from
Cork to Sligo ?

Answer _____ kms   [1]

b.   What is the distance from
Belfast to Limerick ?

Answer_____ kms   [1]

c.   The Delivery lorry leaves Dublin
to make deliveries in Cork and Limerick
before returning directly to Dublin.
What is the total distance of the journey ?

Answer _____ kms   [2]

d.   What is the total distance if the lorry
leaves Belfast and makes deliveries in
Sligo, Limerick, Cork and Dublin and
then returning to Belfast ?

Answer_____ kms   [2]

4. The Pie chart represents the colours of flags used at a Motor Racing track.

B--black

C--chequered

R--red

G--green

Y--yellow

a. Which is the most common colour ?

Answer _____ [1]

b. What percentage of the flags are Yellow ?

Answer _____ % [1]

c. Which colour represents 15% of the flags ?

Answer _____ [2]

d. There are 12 black flags.
What is the total number of flags ?

Answer _____ [2]

5. The table shows the time in minutes for a racing car to complete various numbers of laps of a circuit.

Time in minutes	3	4.5	6	12	13.5
No. of Laps	2	3	4	8	9

a. Using the graph below draw the line graph for this data.

[2]

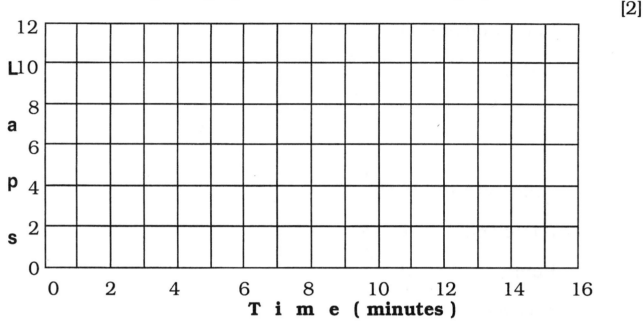

b. How many laps will the car travel in 15 minutes ?

Answer _____ laps

[1]

c. How long will it take for the car to cover 20 laps ?

Answer _____ mins   [1]

d. How many laps will the car travel in an hour ?

Answer _____ laps   [1]

e. How many minutes will it take the car to travel 1 lap ?

Answer_____ mins   [1]

6. Countries across the world have different time zones as shown in the diagram below.
Time is measured in relation to GMT (Greenwich Mean Time).

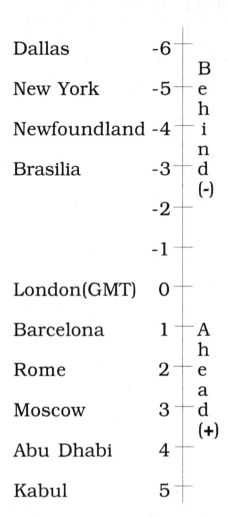

a. What is the difference in time between New York and Kabul ?

Answer _____ hrs   [1]

b. If the time in Barcelona is 1400 what is the time in Dallas ?

Answer _____   [1]

c. A flight leaves London at 0800 for a flight to Newfoundland. The flight takes 6 hours.
At what Newfoundland time does the flight arrive ?

Answer _____   [2]

SHOW ALL YOUR WORKING

7. A cardboard tray for holding building blocks is drawn here.

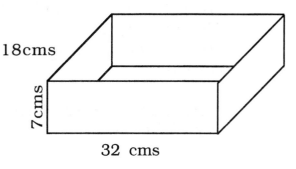

18cms

7cms

32 cms

a. The top is open. Sketch a net of the box.

One side is already drawn.

[2]

b. What is the area of cardboard needed to make this open box ? Show your working .

Answer _____ sq. cms.   [2]

8. Simplify the following.

a.   **3 + 4x - 7 - 2x**

Answer _____   [1]

b.   **3 x 3y + 6 - 4y**

Answer_____   [1]

7.

SHOW ALL YOUR WORKING

9.   The diagram has parallel lines AB and CD and a line EF crossing them.
The size of one angle is shown.

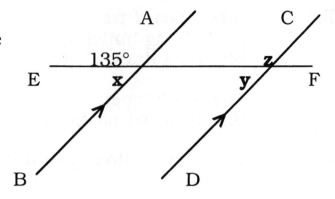

a.   Work out the size of the angles below .

Answer   **z** = _____ °   [1]

x = _____ °   [1]

y = _____ °   [1]

b.   What name is given to the pair of angles **x** and **y** ?

Answer _____   [1]

10.   Below is a number sequence. The first 4 numbers are :-

a,   a + 2,   a + 4,   a + 6, ...

Write down the next 3 terms.

a.   Answer_____,   _____, _____.   [1]

b.   What is the SUM of the these 3 terms.

Answer _____   [2]

c.   What is the PRODUCT of the first 2 terms.

Answer _____   [2]

8.

11. The Table below represents a TV monitor in the lounge of Belfast International Airport.

Flight No.	Destination	Dep.Time	Arr. time
BA75	Amsterdam	0710	1005
BM95	Rome	0745	1040
VA80	Atlanta	0750	1740
BA99	Sydney	0800	2130
BM90	Madrid	0825	1115
AA55	New York	0855	1540

a. How long does the flight from Belfast to Madrid take ?

Answer_____ hrs _____ mins   [1]

b. How much longer does the flight from Belfast to Atlanta take than the flight from Belfast to New York ?

Answer _____ hrs _____ mins   [1]

c. Alice and her sister Yvonne boarded different flights, Alice to Rome and Yvonne to Madrid. Each promised to ring the other immediately when **both had landed.**
At what time did the two sisters ring each other ?

Answer _____   [2]

9.

12.   The table shows the Exchange Rates for 4 Foreign countries.

USA.................................   1 . 60 Dollars for £1 sterling

Mexico.............................   14 . 3 Pesos for £1 sterling

Switzerland......................   2 . 3 Francs for £1 sterling

Japan.............................   180 yen for £1 sterling

a.   Ann is going on holiday to
Mexico and wants to change £280.
How many Pesos does she get ?

Answer_____ Pesos   [1]

b.   A family went to the USA and changed
£600 into dollars.
How many dollars did they get for £600 ?

Answer _____ Dollars   [1]

c.   On returning from holiday the father had
to go to Switzerland on business.
He had 640 dollars left, so he went into
the bank to get the dollars changed to
Swiss francs. The bank teller first changed
the dollars to pounds sterling and then
to francs.
How many francs did he get ?

Answer_____ Swiss francs   [2]

d.   After returning from Japan James had
8100 yen and she changed them back
to pounds sterling.
How much did she get in £ sterling ?

Answer £ _____   [1]

13. The following sequence is set as a teaser for a third year class. The pupils are asked to work out a rule for the sequence.

1,   8, ...

a. Mary worked out the following rule :-
"**multiply the previous number by 3 and add 5**".

Write in the next 3 numbers.

Answer **1, 8,** _ _ __ __ _,   _ _ __ __ _,   _ _ __ __ _.

[1]

b. Harry figures that the rule should be :-
"**1st number is 1 cubed, 2nd number is 2 cubed and so on...**"

Write in Harry's next 3 numbers.

Answer **1, 8,** _ _ __ __,   _ _ __ __ _,   _ _ __ __ _.

[1]

c. A Third Rule involving **MULTIPLYING** and **SUBTRACTING** the sequence number will give the following sequence.

Sequence Number	1	2	3	4	5
	1,	8,	15,	22,	29.

Write down this RULE._____

_____ [2]

14. Which of the following is the **best estimate** for this decimal sum.

0.9 x 11.06 x 9.6

Circle your answer.

150   90   100   990

[1]

11.

SHOW ALL YOUR WORKING

15. When a Survey of a car park was taken at a particular time the number of each of the following colours was recorded in the table below.

Colour of cars	Black	Yellow	Brown	Red	White
Number	40	80	40	160	80

a. What was the **total** number of cars ?

Answer_____ cars   [1]

b. What was the **modal** colour of car ?

Answer _____   [1]

c. The Pie-chart shows one of the colours. Write the colour in the box provided .

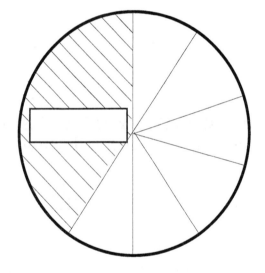

[1]

d. Complete the Pie-chart for the other colours and label each sector.   [2]

e. What percentage of cars were **White** ?

Answer_____ %   [1]

f. What was the **Ratio** of RED cars to BROWN cars ?

Answer_____:_____   [1]

PTQ Tuition
Practice Materials
Tel: 02879632342

KEY STAGE 3 MATHEMATICS Paper 3

PRACTICE TEST ③

Time :

Total time for this test is 1 hour.

Instructions :

Write your name in the space below.
Write your answers in the spaces
provided in the paper.
Check your work carefully.

Information :

Total mark for this Test is 66.
Numbers in brackets at the end of
each question indicate the marks awarded
to each answer or part of an answer.

Mark	
Total	66 (Maximum)

Pupil Name :

_____

1.   An unknown number is represented by the letter **t**.

If **t - 6 = 3** :-

a.   What is the number value of **t** ?

Answer _____   [1]

b.   What is the number value of **3t - 13** ?

Answer _____   [1]

c.   What is the **square root** of **t** ?

Answer _____   [1]

2.   Find the value of the following.

a.   -7 + 3 + 2(7 - 2) - 2

Answer _____   [1]

b.   5 - 3(7 - 3) + 8

Answer _____   [1]

3.   Draw lines to match the expressions on the left with the appropriate expression on the right.

                     8rs

a.   2r + 4s

                     6rs

                     $8r^2$

b.   2r x 4s

                     4s + 2r

                     rs

c.   2r x 4r

                     6r   [3]

SHOW ALL YOUR WORKING

4. A survey was carried out in a primary school to determine the popularity of 4 different Sweet bars. The Pie-chart represents the outcome of the survey.

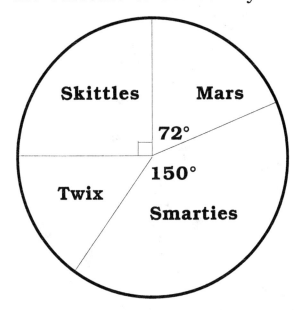

a. What fraction of the total bars is represented by Smarties ?

Answer _____ [2]

b. Which sweet is represented by 25% of the Pie-chart ?

Answer _____ [1]

c. What percentage of the chart is represented by Mars ?

Answer _____ [2]

d. What is the size of the angle represented by Twix ?

Answer _____° [1]

e, In total there are 300 bars. How many of these are Twix ?

Answer _____ [2]

3.

5. The Regular Octagon has diagonals drawn on it.

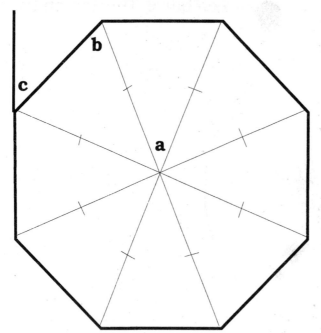

Drawing not to scale.

Calculate the sizes of the following angles.
Show your working.

a. Answer **a** = _____ ° [1]

b. **b** = _____ ° [1]

c. **c** = _____ ° [2]

6. In Jars of sweets there are 3 varieties, Gums, Jellies and Toffees. The Ratio of Gums to Jellies to Toffees is **2 : 3 : 1**.

a. The largest Jar has a total of 210 sweets.
How many of these are **Jellies** ?

Answer _____ jellies [1]

b. A smaller jar has 10 **Toffees**.
What is the overall **total** in this jar ?

Answer _____ sweets [2]

c. The smallest jar has 24 **Jellies.**
How many **Gums** are in this jar ?

Answer _____ gums. [1]

7. Which of the following is the **best estimate** for this decimal sum.

99 x 11 x 0.9

Circle your answer.

10,000   100   1000   10

[1]

8. The 4 Answers shown are the exact answers to the sums shown.
By Rounding the numbers and finding **estimated answers** match up the Sums with their correct answers.
Show your working and use **lines** to match Sums to Answers.

SUMS	ANSWERS
3.09 x 19.8	1209.02
9.3 x 11.42	61.182
99.1 x 12.2	28.71
0.99 x 29	106.206

[3]

9. Look at the following Function Machine.

3	SUBTRACT 2 MULTIPLY BY 3	3
5		_____
7		_____
11		_____
_____		48
_____		63

Fill in the missing numbers.   [2]

5.

SHOW ALL YOUR WORKING

10. Simplify the following algebraic expressions :-

a. $- 4p + 3p + 2p = $ _____

b. $4x - 3y - 2x + 2y = $ _____

c. $b^2 + b + b^2 + b = $ _____ [3]

11. The first 4 numbers of a sequence are shown below.

Write in the next two numbers of the sequence. [1]

$0.4, \ 0.6, \ 1.0, \ 1.8,$ _____ , _____ .

12. Look at the square.

Its dimensions are shown

in centimetres.

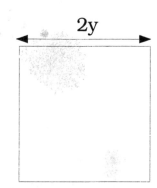

a. Write down in terms of **y** a formula
for the Perimeter, **P** of this square.

Answer **P** = _____ [1]

b. If the Perimeter of this square is
64 cms what length is the square ?

Answer _____ cms [1]

c. What is the area in square metres
of this square ?

Answer _____ sq. cms. [1]

6.

1. a. 8 **b.** 64 **c.** 1
2. 8 →**23, 12** ←35, **37** ←110
3. a. Stew and Roll
3. b. Soup, Burger and Chips **c.** £12.41
4. a. 30th **b.** Saturday **c.** 6th
                    5. a. ——————→

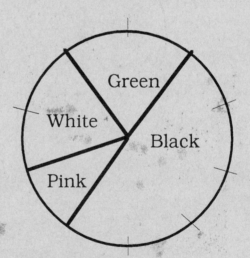

5. b. 270°
6. a. 210 **b.** 167
7. a. 77 **b.** 244
8. a. 7 **b.** 119
9. a. 47
b. Double the difference between the 2 previous terms
10. A--17, B--45, C--32, D--20
11. a. 4.56 cms **b.** 0.9 cms **c.** 308 cms **d.** 54 cms
12. a. 60 **b.** 63 **c.** 240
13. a. 3 inches **b.** 30 cms
14. a. 0.11 **b.** 70
15. a. 100 **b.** 1000
16. 2.2 kgs
17. a. £49.68 **b.** £87.80
18. a. 16 **b.** 8, 10, 20, 40 **c.** 37
19. a. Scooter, 19kms **b.** 20 litres
20. a. 15750 grams **b.** 4375 grams
    c. 8 kgs **d.** 3635 grams
21. D
22. £0.65
23. a. 1205 **b.** 2030 **c.** 4hrs 15mins
    d. 1735 **e.** 2hrs 40 mins
24. Green is 2 sections like white;
    Pink is 1 section while
    Black is the largest section.

1. a. 10 **b.** 33 **c.** 1000
2. a. 2 : 3 **b.** 40% **c.** 480
3. a. 190 kms **b.** 250 kms **c.** 490 kms **d.** 841 kms
4. a. yellow **b.** 30%
4. c. red **d.** 60
5.a. ——————→

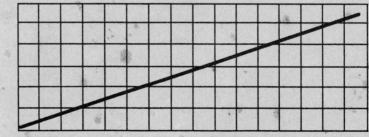

5. b. 10 laps **c.** 30 mins   **d.** 40 laps **e.** 1.5 mins
6. a. 10 hrs **b.** 07:00   **c.** 10:00
7. a.

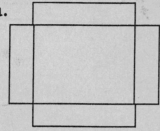

7.b. 1276sq. cms.

8. a. 2x - 4 **b.** 5y + 6
9. a. z = 135°, x = 45°, y = 45° **b.** corresponding
10. a. a + 8, a + 10, a + 12   **b.** 3a + 30 **c.** a^2 + 2a
11. a. 2hrs 50mins **b.** 3hrs 5mins   **c.** 11:15
12. a. 4004 pesos **b.** $960   **c.** 920 francs **d.** £45
    13. a.   29, 92, 281. **b.** 27, 64, 125.
    c. Multiply sequence number by 7, then subtract 6.
        (1 x 7 - 6 = 1. 2 x 7 - 6 = 8, 3 x 7 - 6 = 15,
        4 x 7 - 6 = 22, 5 x 7 - 6 = 29
14. ⟨100⟩
15. a. 400 cars **b.** red **c.** red
15. d.   **brown**

e. 20%
f. 4 : 1

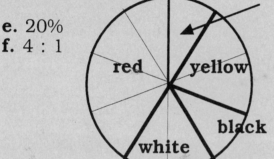

Paper 3   **ANSWERS**   **Test 3.**

1. a. 9 **b.** 14 **c.** 3
2. a. 4 **b.** 1
3. a. 2r + 4s ⟶ 4s + 2r   **b.** 2r x 4s ⟶ 8rs
    c. 2r x 4r ⟶ $8r^2$
4. a. 5 twelfths   **b.** Skittles **c.** 20% **d.** 48° **e.** 40
5. a = 45° **b.** b = 67.5° **c.** c = 45°
6. a. 105 jellies **b.** 60 sweets **c.** 16 gums
7. 1000
8. 3.09 x 19.8 ⟶ 61.182, 9.3 x 11.42 ⟶ 106.206
    99.1 x 12.2 ⟶ 1209.02, 0.99 x 29 ⟶ 28.71
9. 5 ⟶ **9**, 7 ⟶ **15**, 11 ⟶ **27**,
    18 ⟵ 48, **23** ⟵ 63.
10. a. p **b.** 2x - y **c.** $2b^2$ + 2b
11. 3.4, 6.6
12. a. P = 8y **b.** 16 cms **c.** 256 sq. cms.

13. a.

Hrs	2	3.5	5	6.5	8
Price		£35	£50	£65	£80	£95

13.b.

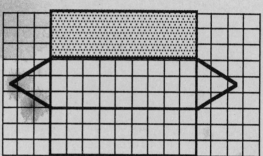

C

13. c. £145
d. 30.5 hrs
e. £553.50

14. a. 12°C
b. 11°C

c. 4°C
d. -12°C

15. a.

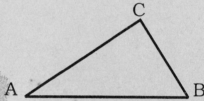

15.b. 355 sq. cms.
16. a. 166 **b.** 165
17. a. a **b.** e **c.** d & g
18. 3 kms.p.h.
19. a. Line BC = 10cms,
line AB = 6 cms and
line AC = 8 cms
b. 53° **c.** 90°

C

A   B

Papers 4/5   **ANSWERS**   **Test 4.**

1. a. 3 x 7 x 11 x 13 **b.** 77
2. a. 7 **b.** 7 **c.** 4 **d.** 1 third **e.** 0
3. a. 230° **b.** 050°
4. 1.2 metres
5. a. Bingo = 50° , Crunchie = 90°, KitKat = 85°,
Picnic = 75°, Twix = 60°.
b. Full marks for all angles correct.
6. a. $3(a - 3b + 5)$ **b.** $3x^2 (3x + x^2 - 2)$
7. a. 1000°C and -50°C **b.** 1050°C **c.** -9°C and -0°C
d. 9°C **e.** -34°C
8. 24.9
9. a. CGA = 40°, AEG = 70°. **b.** AFG = 40°, AGD = 140°.
c. GFB = 140°, EGF = 30° .
10. £1460
11. a. 47.5 cms **b.** 4.5 cms
12. a. a^6 **b.** 1 **c.** $4p^8$
13. a.

G,B	G,Y	G,G	G,R
R,B	R,Y	R,G	R,R
B,B	B,Y	B,G	B,R

13. b. 0   **c.** 3 quarters   **d.** 1 half   **e.** 6
14. a. B   **b.** -2   **c.** becomes bigger   **d.** becomes smaller
15. a. 13 cms   **b.** 15 cms
     c. Length=19 cms, Width=17 cms, Height=13 cms
16. a. 15 kgs   **b.** 10.5 kgs
17. 25%
18. 7 tenths
19. Mean = 26,   Median = 22, Mode = 13.

Papers 4/5   **ANSWERS**   **Test 5.**

1. a. AB = 12.4 cms   **b.** BC = from 8.79 to 8.82
2. a. £335   **b.** 100 tonnes
3. a.

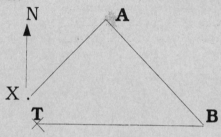

3. b. 315
4. 15%
5. a. 90 km.p.h.   **b.** 84kmph   **c.** 176kms
6. a. (7 - 3) x 13 - 9   **b.** (7 - 3) x (13 - 9)
7. a. £4   **b.** £8.20   **c.** £3 + 10x pence
8. £20%
9. a. C = (2, -4)   D = (-1,-2)
9. b. E = (2,0)   **c.** Isosceles   **d.** 18 sq.cms
10. a. 3 tenths   **b.** 8 tenths or 4 fifths   **c.** 3 tenths   **d.** 200

11. a. $x = 35°$ **b.** $y = 65°$ **c.** $w = 100°$ **d.** $z = 35°$
12. a. $x = 2.5$
12. b. $d = 3$ **c.** $p = 6$
13. a. $4y \leq 8 - x$ **b.** $x \leq 5$ **c.** $x \geq -2$ **d.** $y \geq -2$
14. a. 538.51 cubic cms   **b.** 1769.88 cubic cms
15. a. 13 x 7 x 3 x 5   **b.** 91
16. a. £450   **b.** £126
17. Mean = 1255,   Median = 1223,   Mode = 1134

18. a.

x	-3	-2	-1	0	1	2	3
$y = 3 - x^2$	(-6)	-1	(2)	(3)	2	(-1)	-6

   b. Full marks for all correct co-ordinates and
     smooth parabolic curve.
   c. Full marks for correct straight line graph.
   d. (-2,-1), (2, -1)

SHOW ALL YOUR WORKING

13. A Plumber has to use a Formula to work out what he has to charge for a job. He uses the following :-

| Call-out charge £15 | + | Cost per hour £10 | = | Total Price |

a. Complete the table below for the Plumber's Prices. [2]

Hours	2	3.5	5	6.5	8
Price					

b.   Complete the Graph below starting from point **C**. [2]

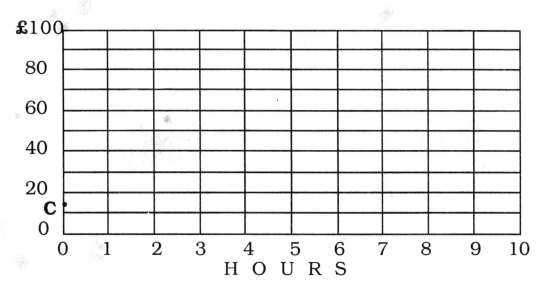

c. Using the table and the graph calculate
the total cost of a job which lasts 13 hours .

Answer £_____ [1]

d. For how many hours does a job which
costs £320 last ?

Answer _____ hours [2]

e. For any job over 30 hours the plumber
gives a 10% discount.
Calculate the price of a job which lasts 60 hours ?

Answer £_____ [2]

7.

SHOW ALL YOUR WORKING

14. Different cities have different Winter temperatures. The diagram below shows a number of world cities and their Celsius temperatures in December.

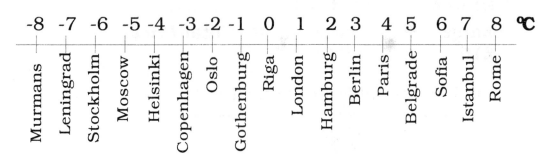

a. By how many degrees is the Leningrad temperature different than the temperaure in Belgrade ?

Answer _____°C   [1]

b. What is the difference between the temperature in Rome and the temperature in Copenhagen ?

Answer _____°C   [1]

c. If the Helsinki temperature rises by 8 degrees what is the new temperature ?

Answer _____°C   [1]

d. If the temperature in Helsinki falls by 8 degrees what is the new temperature ?

Answer _____°C   [1]

8.

SHOW ALL YOUR WORKING

15.   Here is a drawing of
a triangular prism
made from thin metal.

a.   Using the grid below
draw the net of the
prism and mark on it
the patterned side.

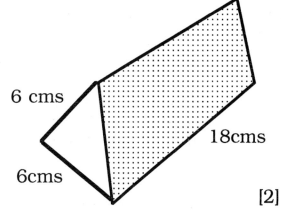

6 cms

6cms

18cms

Scale : 1 square = 2 cms   [2]

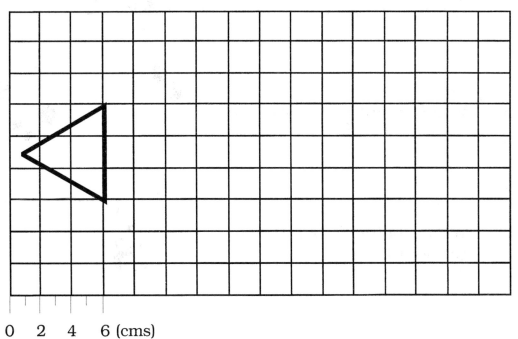

0   2   4   6 (cms)

b.   What is the total area of metal needed to make
this net, to the nearest square centimetre?

Answer _____ sq.cms.   [2]

16.   Use the calculation in the box
to fill in the answers below.

$$75 \times 166 = 12450$$

a.   150 x _____ = 24900   [1]

b.   75 x _____ = 12375   [2]

17. The drawing is of a net of a triangular prism.

The letters **a, b, c, d, e, f** and **g** are marked on the drawing.

When the net is folded to form a prism answer the following questions.

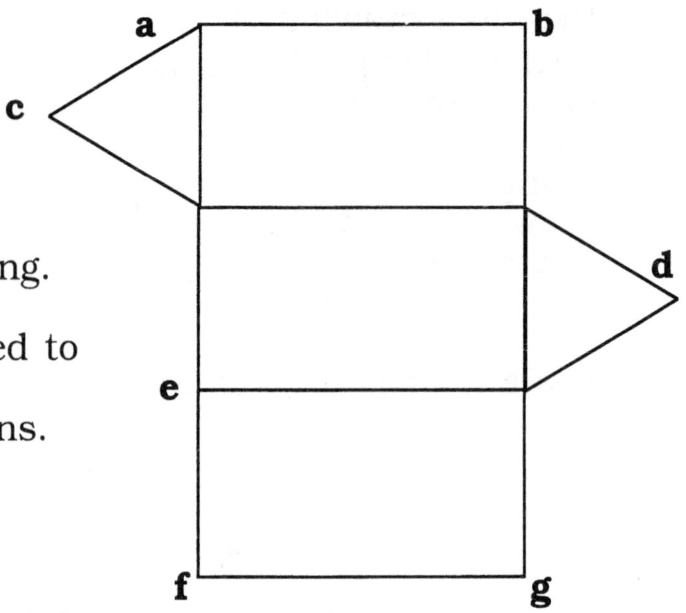

a.   Which point or points join up with **f** ?

Answer _____ [1]

b.   Which point or points join up with **c** ?

Answer _____ [1]

c.   Which point or points join up with **b** ?

Answer _____ [1]

18. John left home at 8.40 am and walked 0.75 kms to school.

He arrived at 8.55 am.

What was Tom's mean speed in kms per hour ?

Answer _____ kms. per hour [2]

10.

19.   Below is a drawing of a Triangle.

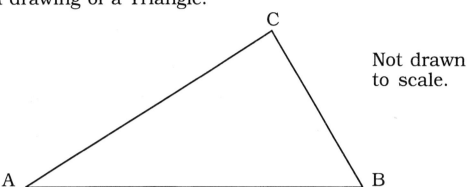

Not drawn to scale.

The following are the lengths of the sides.

AB = 10 cms,   AC = 8 cms and CB = 6 cms.

a.   Starting at point B draw accurately full size the Triangle ABC.

. B

[2]

b.   Measure the internal angle ABC to the nearest degree.

Answer B = _____°   [1]

c.   What can you say
about the angle at C ?

Answer _____   [1]

11.

PTQ Tuition
Practice Materials
Tel: 02879632342

KEY STAGE 3 MATHEMATICS Paper 4/5

PRACTICE TEST 4

Time :

Total time for this test is 1 hour.

Instructions :

Write your name in the space below.
Write your answers in the spaces
provided in the paper.
Check your work carefully.

Information :

Total mark for this Test is 66.
Numbers in brackets at the end of
each question indicate the marks awarded
to each answer or part of an answer.

Mark	
Total	66 (Maximum)

Pupil Name :

_____

1. a.   Given that the value of **13 x 11 x 7 = 1001** express

3003 as a product of its prime factors.

Answer = _____   [1]

b.   Given that **385 = 5 x 7 x 11**, write down the highest common factor (HCF) of **3003** and **385**.

Answer = _____   [2]

2.   On the Saturday before Christmas 2000, the number of cards delivered by a postman to 12 houses in a street was :-

9   11   7   3   4   13   10   7   4   4   8   4

a.   Calculate the **mean** number of
cards delivered to each house.   _____ letters   [2]

b.   Work out the **median** number
of cards delivered to each house.   _____ letters   [1]

c.   Write down the **modal** number
of cards delivered to each house.   _____ letters   [1]

d.   One house is chosen at random.
What is the **probability** that the
house chosen had **exactly 4 cards**
delivered on that day?
Give your answer as a fraction
in its lowest terms .   _____   [2]

e.   What is the **probability** that the
house chosen had **only 2 cards**
delivered that day ?   _____   [1]

3. The diagram shows the position of two towns on a map. The angle with the horizontal is 40 degrees.

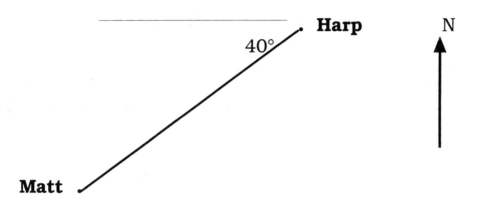

a. Calculate the three figure bearing of Mart from Harp.

_____° [1]

b. Calculate the three figure bearing of Harp from Mart.

_____° [1]

4. The side view of a rubbish skip is drawn below.

The shape is symmetrical. ***Drawing not to scale***

Calculate the height **h** .

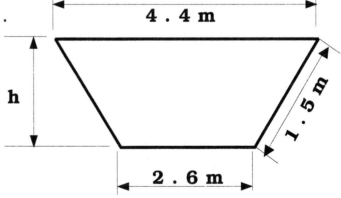

Answer : **h** = _____ metres [2]

5. A survey was carried out in a large Primary school to determine the popularity of chocolate bars.

Five bars Picnic, KitKat, Crunchie, Twix and Bingo were used.

The table shows the result of the pupils' preferences.

Chocolate Bars	No. of Pupils	Angle in Pie chart
Bingo	100	
Crunchie	180	
KitKat	170	
Picnic	150	
Twix	120	

a. Complete the table above working out the angles needed to draw a Pie chart showing the pupils' choices.

[2]

b. Draw the Pie chart below.

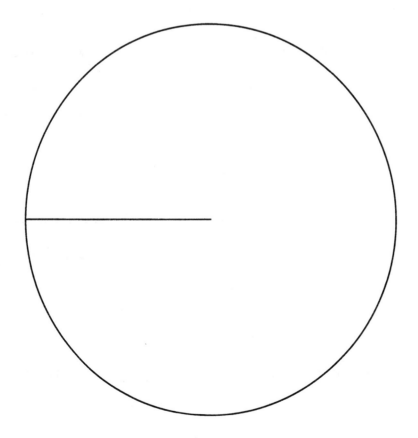

[2]

4.

6. Factorise the following :

a. $3a - 9b + 15$

Answer _____ [1]

b. $9x^3 + 3x^4 - 6x^2$

Answer _____ [1]

7. The table below shows the temperatures of a number of situations.

FREEZING POINT	0°C
ANTARCTIC ICEBERG	- 50°C
BOILING WATER	100°C
MOLTEN GLASS	1000°C
COLD WINTER NIGHT	- 9°C
HOT METAL IN FURNACE	500°C

a. Between which two temperatures is the difference in temperatures the **greatest** ? _____°C and _____°C [1]

b. What is this difference ? _____°C [1]

c. Between which two temperatures is the difference in temperature the **least** ? _____°C and _____°C [1]

d. What is this difference ? _____°C [1]

e. If the temperature of the antarctic iceberg rises by 16 degrees what will the new temperature be ? _____°C [1]

8. Calculate the size of angle **A** in the triangle below.

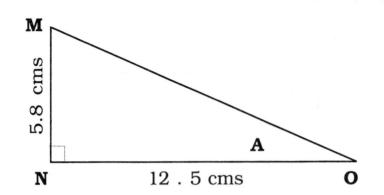

Drawing not

to scale.

MN = 5 . 8 cms and NO = 12 . 5 cms

Give your answer to **3 significant figures**.

Answer :   **A** = _____° [2]

9. In the diagram below the lines AB and CD are parallel.

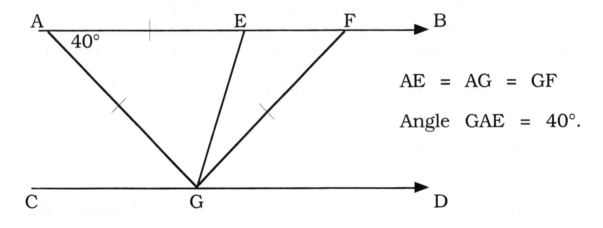

AE = AG = GF

Angle GAE = 40°.

Calculate the following angles.

a.   Angle CGA = _____°   Angle AEG = _____° [1]

b.   Angle AFG = _____°   Angle AGD = _____° [1]

c.   Angle GFB = _____°   Angle EGF = _____° [1]

SHOW ALL YOUR WORKING

10. There is a reduction of 21% in a man's salary for Income tax.

His take-home monthly salary is £1153 . 40.

Calculate his gross monthly salary before Income tax is deducted.

Answer £ _____   [2]

11. The level of water in a reservoir increases as the amount of rainfall increases . The formula used is :-

D = 10R + 25   where **D** = depth of water in cms
and **R** = Rainfall in cms per week.

a. By how much does the Depth of water increase when the week's rainfall was 2 . 25 cms.?   _____ cms   [1]

b. How much rainfall was there at the end of a week when the depth of water had increased by 70 cms ?   _____ cms   [2]

12. Simplify

a. $a^2 \times a^4 \div (a^3 \times a^{-3})$ Answer _____   [1]

b. $s^8 \times s^{-2} \div (s^2)^3$ Answer _____   [1]

c. $(2p^4)^2$ Answer _____   [1]

7.

13.   Two spinners are used for a game.

Spinner X is divided into
4 equal parts and coloured
Blue, Yellow, Green and Red.

Spinner Y is divided into
3 equal parts and coloured
Green, Red and Blue.

a.   Complete the table showing
all possible outcomes.

	SPINNER A			
	Blue	**Yellow**	**Green**	**Red**
Green	G,B			
Red				R,R
Blue				

[2]

What is the probability that, when Spinner A and Spinner B
are each spun ONCE, the following would happen.

b.   **Both** Spinners show **Yellow**.   _____   [1]

c.   **Both** Spinners show **different** colours.   _____   [1]

d.   **Neither** Spinner shows **Green**.   _____   [1]

e.   If the two Spinners are spun
together 24 times **how many times**
are they likely to show the **same** colour.   _____   [1]

8.

SHOW ALL YOUR WORKING

14.   The equation of a reciprocal function is $y = \dfrac{1}{\text{-}x}$

a.   Which diagram represents the graph of the function $y = \dfrac{1}{\text{-}x}$

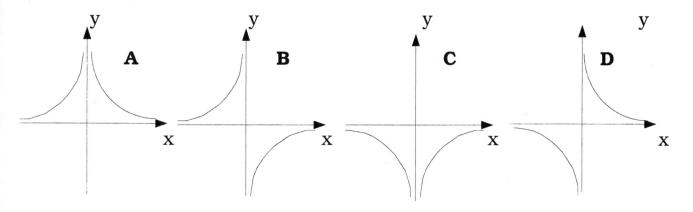

Answer _____   [2]

b.   What is the value of **y** when $x = \dfrac{1}{2}$?

Answer   **y** = _____   [2]

c.   As the value of **x** gets closer to zero
what happens to the value of **y** ?

Answer _____   [1]

d.   As the value of **x** becomes bigger and bigger
what happens to the value of **y** ?

Answer _____   [1]

15. a. The Volume of a cube is **2197** cubic cms.

Work out the length of one side .

Answer _____ cms [2]

b. The Volume of a Hexagonal prism is **570** cubic cms.

The Area of the Hexagonal end is 38 sq. cms.

What is the Length of the prism ? _____ cms. [2]

c. The Volume of a Cuboid is **4199** cubic cms.

The 3 dimensions of the cuboid are two-digit
prime numbers less than 20.
Calculate the 3 dimensions.

Length = _____ cms [1]

Width = _____ cms [1]

Height = _____ cms [1]

16. A cook uses flour, butter and sugar in the Ratio of **3 : 2 : 1**
when making pastry.

a. If the cook uses 5 kg of butter what is
the total weight of Pastry made ? _____ kgs. [1]

b. When making apple pies the cook
needs 21 kg of pastry.
What weight of flour does she need ? _____ kgs. [1]

SHOW ALL YOUR WORKING

17. The Manufacturer's recommendation for the price of a new Toyota car is **£12,000**.
At the end of the season a dealership decides to have a sale and reduces the price of the car.
A regular customer of the dealer is able to agree a further 12 % reduction on the sale price.
He pays **£7875** for the Toyota.

Calculate the original **% reduction** .

Answer _____%   [2]

18. A large Computer company employ a total of 1200 people. They were asked whether or not they wanted to change the parking arrangements at the company.

Of the 1050 employees who replied four fifths said that they wanted to change.

What fraction of **all** the employees wanted to change the parking arrangements ?

Give your answer as a fraction in its lowest form.

Answer _____   [2]

19. Calculate the mean,median and mode of the following numbers.

22,   39,   13,   9,   13,   49,   37.

Answer : Mean   =   _____   [1]

Median   =   _____   [1]

Mode   =   _____   [1]

   11.

PTQ Tuition
Practice Materials
Tel: 02879632342

KEY STAGE 3 MATHEMATICS Paper 4/5

PRACTICE TEST 5

Time :
Total time for this test is 1 hour.

Instructions :
Write your name in the space below.
Write your answers in the spaces provided in the paper.
Check your work carefully.

Information :
Total mark for this Test is 66.
Numbers in brackets at the end of each question indicate the marks awarded to each answer or part of an answer.

Mark	
Total	66 (Maximum)

Pupil Name : ____________________

1.   The drawing below is of a triangle ABC.

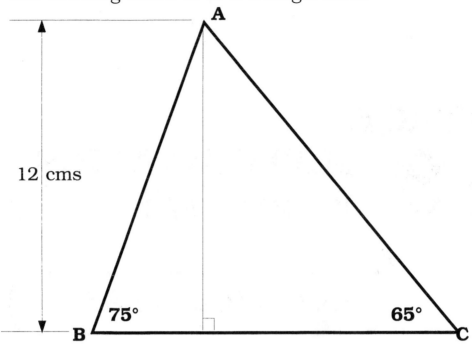

Calculate the length of lines **AB** and **BC**.

Give the answers to **3 significant figures**.

Answer : AB = _____cms   [2]

BC = _____cms   [2]

2.   The Government put a levy on rubbish which is dumped in landfill sites. The formula used by the government is :-

L = 2.5T + 35   where **L** = the Levy in £s
and **T** = weight of rubbish in tonnes.

a.   A building contractor has 120
tonnes of rubbish to dispose.
What levy will be put on this ?   £ _____   [1]

b.   A District Council has a levy of
£285 to pay each week.
How many tonnes of rubbish
does the Council dispose in a week ? _____ tonnes   [1]

2.

3. A Treasure map gave the following instructions for the position of the treasure.

*"From point **X** move 4 km on a bearing of 045° to **A**, then move*

*5 kms on a bearing of 135° to point **B** and finally on a bearing*

*of 270°, move 6 kms to the treasure, **T**. "*

a. Using a scale of **2 cms to 1 km**, draw accurately the path to the treasure, marking points A, B and T.

N

X .

[3]

b. Calculate the Bearing of point A from point B.

Answer _____° [1]

3.

4.   Of a family's household weekly budget of £180, a total of £27 is used for bus fares.

What percentage of the household budget is used for bus fares ?

_____ %   [1]

5.   The distance from Belfast to Mark's home is 45 kms. It takes mark 30 minutes to drive home.

a.   Calculate in kilometres per hour his **average speed** for the journey .   _____ km.p.h.   [1]

b.   He continues the journey to his brother's house, a distance of 60 kms. It takes him another 45 minutes. Calculate in kilometres per hour the average speed for the **whole journey**.

_____ km.p.h.   [1]

c.   The next day Mark drives for 2 hours and 40 mins at an average speed of 66 km.p.h.

What is the **total** distance of this journey ?

_____ kms.   [1]

6.   Place brackets in the following mathematical statements to make them true.

a.   **7 - 3 x 13 - 9 = 43**   [1]

b.   **7 - 3 x 13 - 9 = 16**   [1]

7. To encourage John to save his parents decide to increase his pocket money by 10 pence at the end of each week.

John starts off with pocket money of £3.00.

Each week after this his pocket money increases by 10 pence.

a. How much pocket money will John get at the end of another 10 weeks ?

Answer £ _____ per week [1]

b. How much will John get at the end of a year ?

Answer £ _____ [1]

c. How much pocket money will John get at the end of x - weeks ?

Answer **£ 3 +** _____ [2]

8. A greengrocer sells 4 boxes of apples each week. In each box there are 160 apples. In the 4 boxes last week he found 128 rotten apples.

What percentage of last week's apple order were rotten ?

Show your working.

_____ % [1]

9. On the 1 cm square grid **A** has the co-ordinates **(-1, 2)** and **B** has co-ordinates **(2, 4).**
The **x-axis** is the line of symmetry of the trapezium **ABCD**.

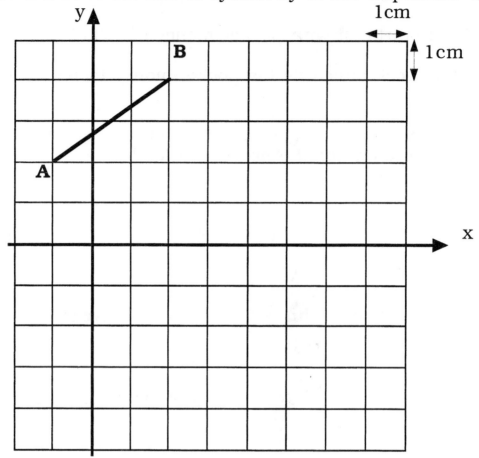

a. What are the co-ordinates of C and D ?

C = (____,____)   D = (____,____)   [2]

b. On the same drawing ADCE is a parallelogram.
What are the co-ordinates of E ?

E = (____,____)   [2]

c. What kind of a triangle is ABE ?

Answer _____   [1]

d. Find the area of trapezium ABCD.

Answer _____ sq. cms.   [2]

10.   The 10-sided spinner below is divided into 10 similar triangles

The triangles are coloured as shown.

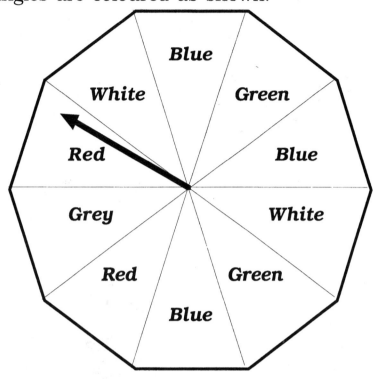

If the spinner is spun once find the probability in fraction form that the arrow will point to a section which is :-

a.   **blue**

Answer _____   [1]

b.   **not green**

Answer _____   [1]

c.   **grey or white**

Answer _____   [1]

d.   The spinner is spun 1000 times.
How many times would the arrow
be expected to point to a **red triangle** ?

Answer _____ times   [2]

11.

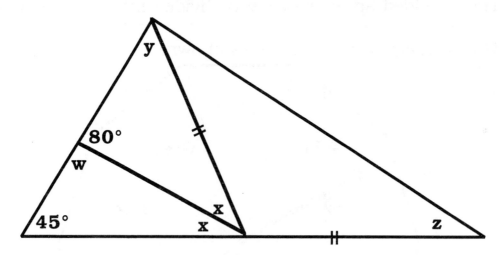

Calculate the value of the following angles :-

a.   **x =** __ ___ _ __ __ _°   [1]   b. **y =** __ ___ _ __ __ __ _°   [1]

c.   **w =** _ ___ __ __ _°   [1]   d. **z =** __ _ __ __ __ __ _°   [2]

12.   Solve the following equations.

a.   **2x - 5 = 10 - 4x**

Answer :   **x =** _____   [1]

b.   **2(2d - 1) + 4 = 2d + 8**

Answer :   **d =** _____   [1]

c.   **4p² - 100 = 44**

Answer :   **p =** _____   [2]

8.

13. The equation of the line PQ in the quadrilateral below is : **4y = 8 - x**

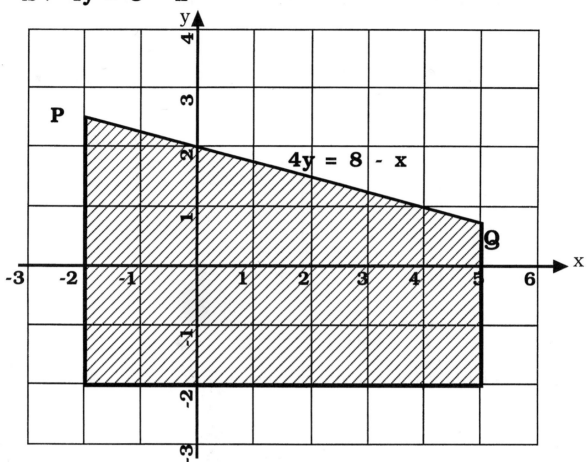

Write down 4 inequalities which will satisfy all the values of **x** and **y** which lie in the shaded region.

a.   Answer : _____

b.   _____

c.   _____

d.   _____

[4]

14. The cylinder below represents a large tin of beans.

The height of the cylinder is 14 cms and the diameter is 7 cms.

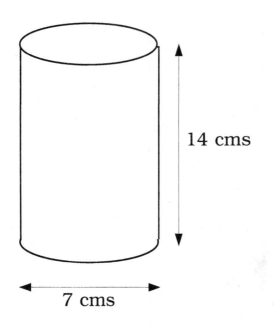

14 cms

7 cms

Drawing is

not to scale.

a. Calculate the volume of this cylinder. π = 3 . 14.

Answer _____ cubic cms. [2]

b. 12 of these tins of beans are packed into a cardboard carton so that they are touching each other and the sides of the carton.

The drawing here shows the arrangement.

The height of the carton is **14 cms**.

Calculate the volume of the space in the carton around the tins, represented by the dotted area.

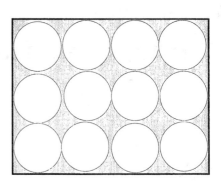

Answer : Volume = _____ cubic cms. [3]

10.

15. a.   Given that the value of **13 x 7 x 3 = 273** express

        1365 as a product of its prime factors.

        Answer = _____   [1]

    b.   Given that **1001 = 13 x 7 x 11**, write down the highest

        common factor (HCF) of **273** and **1001**.

        Answer = _____   [2]

16.   Ann bought a Conservatory on a Hire purchase plan.
The total cost of the Conservatory was £3600.
She paid a deposit of 12 . 5%.

    a.   How much was the deposit ?   £ _____   [1]

    b.   She paid off the balance over 25 months.
What was her monthly payment ?

                               £ _____   [1]

17. Calculate the mean, median and mode of the following numbers.

    1223, 1309, 1134, 1096, 1134, 1502, 1387.

        Answer : Mean   =   _____   [2]

                 Median   =   _____   [1]

                 Mode   =   _____   [1]

18. a. Complete the table for the quadratic function, $y = 3 - x^2$

x	-3	-2	-1	0	1	2	3
$y = 3 - x^2$		-1			2		-6

[2]

b. Draw the graph of the quadratic equation $y = 3 - x^2$

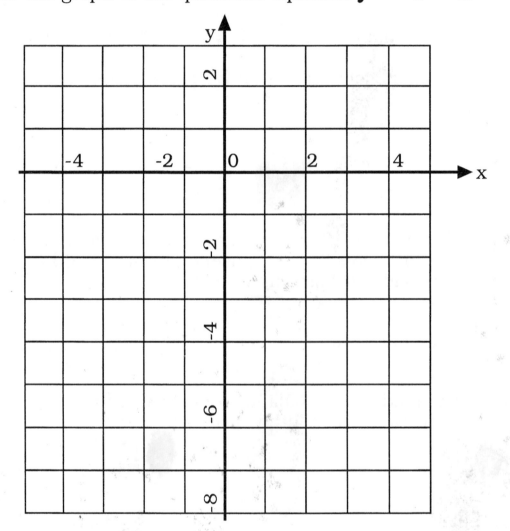

[3]

c. Draw the line graph for the equation $y = -1$. Label it. [1]

d. What are the co-ordinates of points on the graph of the quadratic equation $y = 3 - x^2$ through which the line graph of $y = -1$ passes ?

Answer: (____,____), (____,____). [2]

12.